THE BILL OF RIGHTS

A First Book

THE BILL OF RIGHTS

BY E. B. FINCHER

Franklin Watts / New York / London / 1978

Photographs courtesy of
New York Public Library Picture Collection: p. 7;
The Free Library of Philadelphia: p. 12; Library
of Congress: pp. 24, 49; National Archives/U.S.
Information Agency: p. 25; National Archives/War
Relocation Authority: p. 45 (bottom); United Press
International: pp. 33, 38, 41, 45 (top), 46, 50, 53,
54 (top and bottom).

Library of Congress Cataloging in Publication Data

Fincher, Ernest Barksdale, 1910–
  The Bill of Rights.

  (A First book)
  Bibliography: p.
  Includes index.
  SUMMARY: Discusses how the Bill of Rights
came about and how the people determine how
well these ten amendments to the Constitution are
used.
  1. United States. Constitution. 1st–10th amend-
ments—Juvenile literature. 2. Civil rights—United
States—Juvenile literature. [1. United States Con-
stitution. 1st–10th amendments. 2. Civil rights]
I. Title.
JC599.U5F54   342'.73'085   77–10890
ISBN 0-531-01347-2

CONTENTS

THE BILL OF RIGHTS: SAFEGUARD OF FREEDOM

It seemed that everyone in town had squeezed into the meeting-house. All eyes now turned to the front of the room where a pale young man faced the angry crowd, waiting for a chance to speak. He was there to demand protection from his enemies.

The speaker was Elijah P. Lovejoy, who in 1837 was the editor of a newspaper in Alton, Illinois. He had become highly unpopular because of his views on slavery. Most Americans of that day did not see anything wrong with owning slaves. But Lovejoy dared to tell his countrymen that blacks, no less than whites, had the right to be free. Because he insisted that all men are born free, the young editor was regarded as a troublemaker.

Some months before the town meeting, a gang of men and boys had broken into the building where Lovejoy's newspaper was printed and smashed the press. The leaders of the mob had thought that the young editor would be so frightened that he would leave town. But they underestimated their opponent. He set up another press and continued to print articles that demanded an end to slavery throughout the United States. When a mob destroyed the second printing press, Lovejoy got a third one.

[1]

It was after his third press had been destroyed by the mob that Lovejoy decided the time had come to remind the people of the town that even though his articles made them angry, he had the right to express his views. Not only that—he had the right to be protected from people who were breaking the laws of the United States by destroying his property.

The meetinghouse was a noisy place until the young editor began to speak. Then a great silence settled in the room:

I do not admit that it is the business of this assembly to decide whether I shall or shall not publish a newspaper in this city. . . . I have the right to do it. I know that I have the RIGHT *freely to speak and publish my sentiments, subject only to the laws of the land for the abuse of that right. This right was given me by my Maker; and is solemnly guaranteed to me by the Constitution of these United States and of this state.*

The audience did not like to hear what Lovejoy had to say about the rights given him by God and the Constitution. They liked it even less when he announced that he had ordered a fourth printing press and that he would continue to publish his newspaper.

Lovejoy had several friends at the meeting, and they were moved to tears by his speech. But the great majority of those present were angered by the editor's unwillingness to give up. His opponents took over the meeting, and made it clear that he would not be allowed to print his newspaper.

LOVEJOY'S RIGHTS ARE DEFENDED

Several leading citizens of the town were very disturbed when they realized that Lovejoy could expect no protection from the police.

[2]

They knew that the mob would destroy the new press, as it had destroyed the earlier ones; that is, unless concerned citizens took matters into their own hands.

Not all the citizens who decided to defend Lovejoy agreed with his views on slavery. But to a man, they agreed that the Constitution gave him the right to print what he regarded as the truth.

Lovejoy's supporters armed themselves and made plans to deal with the mob.

Late one night, the new printing press was delivered to a stone warehouse that could be defended. News that Lovejoy had another press swept the town. A mob quickly gathered around the warehouse. The defenders opened the windows wide enough for rifles to show through. Members of the mob realized that the printing press was well defended. Since they could not break down the walls of the warehouse, they decided to set fire to the roof.

Lovejoy saw several men placing a ladder against the wall. He ran outside the warehouse to knock the ladder down. A pistol shot rang out. The young editor fell to the ground.

The mob killed Lovejoy and destroyed his last printing press. But they did not destroy the ideas that he had laid before the people of the town. In fact, Lovejoy had more influence after he died than while he lived. The very fact that a young man had given up his life in defense of his beliefs caused many people to change their views on slavery. And as the report of Lovejoy's death was carried to all parts of the nation, the speech that he had made in defense of his rights was often quoted.

Through his death, Lovejoy reminded Americans that the government of their country is based on two important beliefs: (1) Human beings are born with certain rights that may not lawfully be taken from them, even by the government. (2) From these God-given rights, other rights develop as people live together and work out their differences. To protect citizens from the government that they set up, the rights of persons living in a democratic country are set down in the form of law. Usually these rights are outlined in the constitution, which is a statement that describes the organization of the government. In many cases, the rights of the people are set forth in a special part of the constitution. The Constitution of the United States contains such a section— the Bill of Rights. Elijah P. Lovejoy referred to that part of the Constitution in the last speech that he made. The history and the meaning of that Bill of Rights are the subjects of this book.

EVERY BELIEF
HAS A BEGINNING

"There is nothing new under the sun" is an old saying. It reminds us that everything—including a person's beliefs—has a long history. Certainly Elijah P. Lovejoy's views on human rights did not begin with him. Men and women have talked about their rights from the beginning of time. The young editor was aware of that, having studied history at Colby College in Maine and at Princeton University in New Jersey.

Lovejoy got some of the ideas that he expressed at the public meetings from reading sacred books, such as the Bible and the Koran. Buddha, Jesus, Mohammed, and other religious leaders had much to say concerning the rights that God gives to human beings. And when Lovejoy read about the way the Greeks governed themselves, he learned that citizens enjoyed the right to live freely, without fear of the leaders whom they elected.

But the rules that religious leaders made to keep one individual from taking advantage of another were ignored more often than they were observed. Strong people continued to make slaves of weaker people, to rob them of their property, and to put them to death. And even though sacred books might say that everyone is equal in God's sight, that was not the view held by kings and princes, or by many leaders of the church. On the contrary, the belief developed that kings ruled by divine right, and that ordinary people were required to obey without question those whom God had placed over them.

Powerful rulers sometimes were forced to respect the rights of their people. This happened when the king's subjects joined forces against him. A famous example was the showdown between King John of England and his nobles that occurred in 1215. Over the years, the king had deprived his barons and dukes of what they considered to be their just rights. Finally the nobles organized an army and marched against the king. Once he realized that he would be defeated in battle, King John yielded to his subjects' demands. He signed Magna Carta (Latin words for "Great Charter"), an agreement that is considered a milestone in the history of human freedom. The king agreed to respect his nobles' rights to their property, and to treat his subjects justly.

At first, Magna Carta seemed to be little more than an agreement reached by a king and the richest and most powerful of his subjects. But it was not long before Magna Carta came to mean far more than King John had intended. As time went on, opponents of the English monarchs read new meaning into the words of the agreement. Magna Carta thus became the basis for further checks on the ruler's power and of new safeguards for the rights of the English people. For example, the king's promise not to oppress his subjects came to mean that persons accused of crime could no longer be held in prison as long as the ruler pleased. Instead, they had to be brought before a judge, and reasons given for their arrest and imprisonment. The guilt or innocence

King John was forced to sign Magna Carta in 1215.

[6]

of anyone being tried had to be decided by a jury of the accused person's peers—that is, by a group of citizens chosen to pass judgment. In other words, officials appointed by the king no longer had complete power over someone accused of crime.

Magna Carta became a foundation stone in the system of democratic government that was developing in England. It made plain the fact that the king could not rule as he pleased. He remained the most powerful part of the government, but like his subjects, he had to obey the law.

A CHAIN OF PROMISES

King John was forced to sign Magna Carta almost three hundred years before Columbus discovered the New World, and almost four hundred years before the English established a colony in North America. Yet 1215 is often listed as an important date in the history of the United States. Historians point out that most of the rights enjoyed by the people of this country are based upon promises that English kings were forced to make to their rebellious subjects. The British government reminded Americans of that fact in 1976, the bicentennial year. On the two-hundredth birthday of the United States, the head of the British system of courts, the Lord Chancellor, brought the people of the United States a precious gift—one of the original copies of Magna Carta.

First the great landowners and then the great merchants of England demanded a share in the government. Parliament (a law-making body made up of lords and commoners) was set up. Soon it began to take power from the monarch in the name of the British people. For example, Parliament gained more control over taxes, and it insisted upon helping the king or queen choose public officials.

Meanwhile British judges enlarged the meaning of the agreements that various monarchs made to respect the rights of their subjects. For instance, judges ruled that a citizen's home could not be entered at will by officials of the government, and that when anyone was accused of crime, the person was entitled to a fair trial and just punishment.

But some British rulers attempted to turn back the clock. Their belief that the monarch should be all-powerful caused endless quarrels with Parliament and endless difficulties with the British people. As a matter of fact, it was the interference of the king and his supporters in religious matters that caused the Puritans to come to America. These early settlers wanted to worship God as they thought proper.

Shortly after the first colony was established in Massachusetts, a new king was crowned in London. Charles I and Parliament began to quarrel when the young king tried to control the government. It was not long before King Charles attempted to enforce royal authority with an army. Parliament raised an army of its own, and the king was defeated. In the name of the British people, the leaders of Parliament then forced the king to accept the Petition of Right, which is considered another landmark in the history of freedom. In that agreement, Charles I promised to respect the rights that his people had won through the years.

The king did not hold to the agreement. The war between the royal forces and the army raised by Parliament was resumed. Finally, the king was defeated. He was brought to trial and found guilty of breaking the laws of Great Britain. In 1649, Charles I was beheaded. The whole world was shocked. The people of an important nation had dared to put to death their monarch! The execution seemed to prove that Parliament, which represented the people, was supreme.

For some years, the British government was headed by Oliver Cromwell, a commoner who was backed by Parliament and its army.

Then a monarch was restored to the throne. All went well for a time. But the kings of England had not learned their lesson. Less than fifty years after Charles I was beheaded, Parliament forced another king, James II, from the throne because he attempted to restore the authority that English kings had once enjoyed.

Parliament invited William and Mary, relatives of the former king, to occupy the British throne. But the new rulers had to sign two important papers before they were crowned. In one agreement, they acknowledged the fact that Parliament was supreme, rather than the ruling king or queen. The other paper, the Bill of Rights, required the government to respect the rights of the British people. For example, this important statement protected the citizen's right to own property, to speak and write freely, and to have fair treatment when accused of crime. The Bill of Rights, written in 1689, is important to present-day Americans because it was one of the sources used by the authors of the Constitution of the United States.

A MOST IMPORTANT MEETING

A troop of horsemen rode out to meet the splendid coach as it neared Philadelphia. Cheering people lined both sides of the road, and once the cavalcade reached the city, cannons boomed and church bells rang. George Washington had arrived in the nation's largest city to help work out a new system of government for the United States. The most famous of all Americans was only one of many noted citizens who were coming to Philadelphia for the convention. As newspapers reported the arrival of Alexander Hamilton, James Madison, Rufus King, and other well-known leaders, people realized that a very important meeting was being held in their city.

The delegates to the convention are now called the Founding Fathers because they drew up the Constitution under which the United States has been governed for almost two hundred years. Historians regard the delegates who assembled in 1787 as a very unusual group of men. Most of them were widely read. They were familiar with Magna Carta, the Bill of Rights, and other agreements that had long protected the British people. Moreover, they had read the writings of Greek, Roman, and European authorities on government. Among the

*The Continental Congress laid the
groundwork for the Bill of Rights.*

thinkers who influenced the Founding Fathers was an English writer, John Locke, who lived about one hundred years before the American Revolution. Locke believed that to prevent a government from treating people unjustly, it was necessary to divide its powers among several branches, rather than having authority exercised by one set of officials. In other words, lawmaking should be the responsibility of a legislature, such as Parliament. Carrying out the law should be entrusted to an executive, such as a king or an officer known as the prime, or first, minister. Explaining the meaning of the law should be the duty of the judiciary, or courts. Each of the three branches of government would act as a check on the other two. This would prevent any one of them from having authority enough to deal harshly with the people of a nation.

The Founding Fathers' ideas about government were also influenced by several French writers who lived about the time of the American Revolution. Rousseau (Ru-SEW) believed strongly in the natural rights of human beings. According to Rousseau, these are rights that every person has when born. These rights are not to be taken from a person by any government. "The right to life, freedom, and possessions" is a way of stating the claim that Rousseau made for the human race. Another French writer, Voltaire (Vol-TARE), defended freedom of thought in his books and plays. Throughout his life, Voltaire was the great champion of a person's right to speak freely and to worship without fear of punishment for his or her beliefs.

But the Founding Fathers were men of action, as well as students of the past. Most of them had taken part in the American Revolution, and a number had held important government posts before and after the break with the mother country. They remembered that despite Magna Carta, the Bill of Rights, and other famous agreements, British monarchs had not always respected the rights of their subjects. Even Parliament had deprived the colonists of what they regarded as their just rights.

The mistakes of the past were in the minds of the Founding Fathers when they met in Philadelphia. They did not want to set up a government that would take property without paying for it, forbid citizens to criticize public officials, deny accused persons of a fair trial, or otherwise deprive Americans of rights that their ancestors had won through the centuries.

THE CONSTITUTION: ANOTHER MILESTONE

The delegates to the Constitutional Convention had several goals in mind. First of all, they hoped to establish a government that was strong enough to protect the lives and property of the American people. They knew that when governments cannot maintain order, the rights of all citizens are in danger. A weak government cannot prevent powerful people from taking advantage of defenseless citizens, or honest men and women from being the victims of dishonest ones. And unless the national government is strong, large states can take advantage of small ones.

The Founding Fathers agreed to strengthen the national government by giving Congress, the lawmaking body, far more power than it had under the previous system of government. Next, the authors of the Constitution created a new official—the President of the United States—and gave this Chief Executive a great deal of authority. Then, the Founding Fathers established courts that had the right to decide what was legal according to the Constitution.

The framers of the Constitution realized that a government strong enough to protect the rights of the people can be misused by those who hold office. For that reason, important checks on authority were put into the Constitution, something like the brakes that are provided to keep a powerful automobile under control.

First of all, the Constitution provided for a system of government that was unknown in other countries. Authority was divided between the state governments on the one hand and the federal, or national, government on the other. The plan was to have state power balance federal power. Each state kept its own system of law, its own government, and its own system of taxation. The Constitution drew a boundary between federal authority and state authority. The federal government was to have only those powers given to it by the Constitution. Powers not mentioned there belonged to the states or were retained by the people of the nation.

As a further safeguard, the Founding Fathers followed the advice of John Locke. They divided the powers of the federal government among the President, the Congress, and the courts. Each branch of government was to act as a check on the other. For example, Congress was given the authority to make all national laws, but the President was given the authority to veto, or reject, a proposed law. The President was given the power to enforce the law, but Congress was given the power to remove the President from office in case there was a misuse of authority. And while Congress might pass a law and the President approve it, the Supreme Court was given the right to set the law aside by declaring it unconstitutional. To sum up, the checks-and-balances system was designed to protect civil liberties (another term for human rights). If Congress passed a law that denied those rights, the President could veto the measure. If the President disregarded a civil liberty in an official order, the Supreme Court could declare that the President's action was illegal. And Congress had the power to remove federal judges when they misused their authority.

THE CITIZEN'S RIGHT TO PROTECTION

The Founding Fathers attempted to safeguard the civil liberties of the American people by limiting the power of the federal government and by balancing one branch of government against another. In addition, the Constitution describes particular rights that are to be protected. One of the most important of these is found in the words "the privilege of the writ of habeas corpus shall not be suspended, unless when in cases of rebellion or invasion the public safety may require it." (A writ is a written order given by a judge. "Habeas corpus" is a Latin term that means "You may have the body.") In everyday English, the words put into the Constitution mean that except in time of war or other emergency, a police officer may not arrest someone and keep that person in jail indefinitely and without explanation. The accused person's lawyer, a friend, or a member of the family may ask a judge to issue a writ of habeas corpus. Once the writ is issued, the prisoner must be brought before the judge. At that time, the person under arrest learns the charges against him or her, and friends and family may see that the accused has not been physically harmed. The judge weighs the evidence against the accused person that the police officer produces. Then the judge decides whether the prisoner should be released or held for further investigation.

The writ of habeas corpus is as important a safeguard of human rights now as it was when William and Mary ruled England. Two other safeguards described in the Constitution are rarely needed today, but they are reminders of a time when government officials misused their authority, and brave men and women fought, and sometimes died, in defense of their rights. One of these seldom-needed guarantees forbids Congress to pass a bill of attainder. This means that Congress is denied the right to punish someone by passing a law that takes away the person's property, freedom, or life. Punishment may be inflicted after an accused person has had a fair trial in court, but punishment may not be inflicted simply by passing a law. Some years ago, Congress attempted to use a bill of attainder to punish three federal officials, despite the wording of the Constitution. The three officeholders had angered many members of Congress because of their political beliefs. Congress decided to punish the officials by cutting off their salaries. The case, *United States* v. *Lovett* (1946), was brought before the Supreme Court. The Court declared unanimously that such action was a bill of attainder and therefore unconstitutional. The officials whom Congress had tried to punish received their salaries.

Congress is also forbidden to pass a type of law known as ex post facto (the Latin words mean "from a thing done afterward"). An imaginary example will explain the meaning of the words. Suppose that last year Jane Smith carried a pistol in her car, which was perfectly legal at the time. This year Congress passes a law declaring that anyone who carried a pistol the preceding year can be charged with the crime. In other words, Congress has turned an innocent act into a criminal one simply by passing a law. To put it another way, the government is not allowed to punish a person for something that was not a crime at the time it took place. Moreover, Congress is forbidden to increase the penalty for a crime *after* it has been committed, and to change the rules to make it easier to convict a person accused of crime. These restrictions were placed in the Constitution as protection for those charged with breaking the law.

At one time, anyone who criticized the king or other high official was likely to be accused of treason, which is considered the worst of all crimes because it is directed against the nation itself. The fear of being named as a traitor discouraged many people from speaking freely. Men and women who opposed government officials were often imprisoned and sometimes put to death as traitors. The Founding Fathers wanted to prevent the trial and conviction of persons as traitors merely because they opposed the government. For that reason they described treason very clearly. They limited the meaning of the word to three acts: waging war against the United States, aiding its enemies, or joining them. As a further protection, the Constitution permits conviction for treason only after two or more witnesses have sworn to the traitorous act, or the accused person has confessed in open court.

During the colonial period, it was common practice for Roman Catholics, Jews, and Quakers to be denied the right to vote or to hold office. Even after Independence, some state governments discriminated against various religions. To prevent this practice at the national level, the Constitution declares that one's religion may not bar one from "any office or public trust under the United States."

OPPOSITION TO THE CONSTITUTION

Today Americans are proud of the Constitution, and regard it as almost sacred. It is hard for people now living to realize that when the Founding Fathers presented the newly completed Constitution to their fellow citizens there was great opposition to it. Some of the most notable leaders of the nation promptly announced that they would prevent the ratification, or acceptance, of the Constitution. Patrick Henry of Virginia, John Hancock and Samuel Adams of Massachusetts, and George Clinton of New York were among the leaders of the opposition. They were convinced that the system of government described in the Constitution threatened the freedom of the American people. The government that the Founding Fathers wanted to establish was too powerful. Having escaped the oppression of King George and the British Parliament, Patrick Henry and those who shared his views did not want to be ground down by an all-powerful government established by their fellow Americans.

One of the principal objections to the proposed Constitution was the absence of a bill of rights. Opponents believed that it was not enough to safeguard civil liberties by having one branch of government check the other. There were many precious rights that were not mentioned in the Constitution. Guarantees of those rights would have to be added to the Constitution, or it would be rejected.

For months it appeared that Massachusetts, New York, and Virginia would not accept the Constitution. Since these were three of the most populous states, their rejection of the new system of government would wreck the plans made by the Founding Fathers. The methods that Alexander Hamilton, James Madison, and other supporters of the Constitution used to bring about its adoption are interesting to read about. Opponents of the Constitution were in the majority at the beginning of the ratification campaign. But by using skillful and sometimes sharp practices, defenders of the Constitution managed to bring about its ratification in the key states. In Massachusetts, for example, supporters of the Constitution caused Samuel Adams to change his mind by what some historians have described as a trick. Adams was popular with the cabinetmakers, silversmiths, and other craftsmen of Boston. Supporters of the Constitution felt sure that Adams would accept the new system of government if he believed that the people who kept him in power wanted it. Supporters of the Constitution persuaded Paul Revere to stage a mass meeting of craftsmen in the tavern that Adams had used as headquarters in the early days of the American Revolution. Under Revere's skillful leading, the craftsmen agreed to a strong statement supporting the Constitution. A committee headed by Revere then took the statement to Samuel Adams. Once convinced that his supporters approved of the Constitution, Adams gave up his opposition and agreed to work for ratification. But final acceptance in Massachusetts, as in Virginia and New York, was not assured until Hamilton, Madison, and others who championed the Constitution promised to add a bill of rights to it as soon as the new government was established.

Shortly after the first Congress assembled, proposed amendments, or additions, to the Constitution were drawn up and submitted to the states for their approval. The ten amendments that were ratified by the legislatures of three-fourths of the states were added to the Constitution in 1791. These make up the Bill of Rights.

No less an authority than James Madison, the "Father of the Constitution," promised that the Bill of Rights would force the federal government to behave itself. In other words, the Bill of Rights was meant to serve as a check on the federal government, rather than on the states.

From what possible misdeeds of the federal government did the Bill of Rights protect Americans? In answering that question, attention will be drawn to the background of each of the first ten amendments to the Constitution.

THE BILL OF RIGHTS

THE FIRST AMENDMENT

At the time the government of the United States was set in motion, most European nations had an established, or official, church. That is, one church had a favored position, and it received support from the government in the form of money, as well as privileges—such as control over schools and colleges. In some countries, including England, the monarch was not only the head of the government, but he or she was also head of the established church. Even in the American colonies, the Congregational church was established in Massachusetts, New Hampshire, and Connecticut, while in Virginia it was the Anglican, or Episcopal, church that was supported with public funds.

Americans who were not members of an established church objected to having their taxes used to support a religion other than their own. They regarded the union of church and government as improper because it gave one group of people an advantage over another. Also it allowed public officials to interfere in religious matters, and leaders of the official church to meddle in the affairs of government.

The First Amendment forbade Congress to set up an
official church or otherwise to favor one religion over another.

[21]

Several of the American colonies were founded by men and women who were fleeing from religious persecution, or punishment for their beliefs. But many of those same colonists were not willing to let people of differing religious views live in their midst. Freedom of religion was for members of their faith, but for no one else. The Puritans, for example, punished Quakers by means of whipping, branding with a hot iron, or cutting off an ear. In Pennsylvania, where the Quakers were in control, all those who believed in "one Almighty God" were permitted to live in peace, but only those who believed in "Jesus Christ, the Saviour of the World" could participate in the government. Maryland, founded by Roman Catholics who had been persecuted in England, respected the rights of other Christians, but not the rights of Jews. By the time the United States became a nation, religious toleration, or acceptance, was more widely practiced than during the colonial period. Even so, Jews, Roman Catholics, and nonbelievers were second-class ciitzens in several states.

To prevent Americans from being treated unequally because of their religion, the First Amendment prohibited Congress from interfering with freedom of religion.

At the time the Bill of Rights was drawn up, many Americans regarded free speech as their most important privilege. Freedom to express one's beliefs without fear of punishment has two important aspects, or sides. Free speech is not simply the personal right of an individual to state a fact or express an opinion. It also is the right of everyone else to be able to hear what that person has to say.

Americans who expressed ideas that were not popular got into trouble with colonial officials, particularly when the government itself was criticized. A person who spoke against authority was likely to be fined, placed in the stocks, or jailed. Even after Independence, state officials sometimes curbed free speech when they disapproved of what was being said.

To protect a person's right to speak freely, however unpopular the ideas expressed, the federal government was forbidden to abridge, or restrict, freedom of speech.

Some colonial officials claimed the right to prevent the publication of material that they considered damaging to the government, and to punish editors who dared to print articles that showed disrespect for authority. For example, John Peter Zenger, the publisher of a newspaper in New York City, was brought to trial in 1735 for having criticized an official of the king. The royal government charged that the statements made about the official were libelous. (A legal term for writing that damages a person by blackening the person's character or causing people to ridicule, or make fun of that individual.) Zenger claimed that the government wanted to silence him because he was a very outspoken opponent.

The jury that heard the case decided in favor of Zenger. The famous decision encouraged other editors to criticize the government more freely. A hundred years after Zenger made good his right to criticize the colonial government, Elijah P. Lovejoy made the same claim in attacking the federal government for permitting the enslavement of black Americans.

The First Amendment forbids the federal government to restrict the freedom of the press.

When people feel that they have been unjustly treated by their government, they may protest by writing letters to public officials. Or groups of troubled citizens may try to influence the government by appearing before the capitol or other public building to demand con-

By his Excellency

William Cosby, Captain General and Governour in Chief of the Provinces of *New-York*, *New-Jersey*, and Territories thereon depending in America, Vice-Admiral of the same, and Colonel in His Majesty's Army.

A PROCLAMATION.

Whereas Ill-minded and Disaffected Persons have lately dispersed in the City of *New-York*, and divers other Places, several Scandalous and Seditious Libels, but more particularly two Printed Scandalous Songs or Ballads, highly defaming the Administration of His Majesty's Government in this Province, tending greatly to inflame the Minds of His Majesty's good Subjects, and to disturb the Publick Peace. *And Whereas* the Grand Jury for the City and County of New-York did lately, by their Address to me, complain of these Pernicious Practices, and request me to issue a Proclamation for the Discovery of the Offenders, that they might, by Law, receive a Punishment adequate to their Guilt and Crime. *I Have* therefore thought fit, by and with the Advice of his Majesty's Council, to issue this Proclamation, hereby Promising *Twenty Pounds* as a Reward, to such Person or Persons who shall discover the Author or Authors of the two Scandalous Songs or Ballads aforesaid, to be paid to the Person or Persons discovering the same, as soon as such Author or Authors shall be Convicted of having been the Author or Authors thereof.

GIVEN under My Hand and Seal at Fort-George in New-York this Sixth Day of November, in the Eighth year of the Reign of Our Sovereign Lord George the Second, by the Grace of GOD of Great-Britain, France and Ireland, KING, Defender of the Faith, &c. and in the year of Our LORD, 1734.

By his Excellency's Command,
Fred. Morris, D. Cl. Conc.

W. COSBY.

GOD Save the KING.

*Left: This proclamation was issued
against John Peter Zenger in 1734.
Above: The First Amendment guarantees
the right to protest. This early
protest took place in St. Louis.*

sideration of their complaints. Public officials sometimes regard such gatherings as a show of force, and react angrily, as royal governors frequently did when people assembled in Boston and other cities to protest laws which they considered unjust. But demonstrations against laws that the colonists regarded as unfair sometimes caused the British Parliament to change its policies.

In order to protect the rights of citizens to influence their government by individual or group effort, the First Amendment forbids Congress to pass any law that interferes with "the right of the people peaceably to assemble, and to petition the Government for a redress of grievances."

THE SECOND AMENDMENT

The British soldiers stationed in the American colonies were widely disliked. The redcoats represented the king's authority, and they were used to enforce laws that many citizens considered harsh and unfair. As the thirteen colonies moved toward independence, they set up citizen armies, known as militias, to offset royal military power. These militias became the basis of the Continental Army that George Washington led to final victory. The Second Amendment pays tribute in these words to the part played by the people's army in securing the independence of the United States:

"A well regulated Militia, being necessary to the security of a free State, the right of the people to keep and bear Arms, shall not be infringed."

[26]

THE THIRD AMENDMENT

During the colonial period, it was common practice for the royal government to quarter, or place, soldiers in private homes, and thus to force citizens to provide room and board. Other than requiring colonists to help support the army that defended them, the British government had another reason for quartering soldiers in private homes. The redcoats intimidated, or put in fear, citizens who were opposed to the royal government. How hateful the practice was to the Founding Fathers is indicated in the Third Amendment:

> *"No Soldier shall, in time of peace be quartered in*
> *any house, without the consent of the Owner, nor in*
> *time of war, but in a manner to be prescribed by law."*

THE FOURTH AMENDMENT

Rulers once claimed the unrestricted right to have their officials enter and search the homes of their subjects, to take anything that seemed to indicate the owner was involved in some sort of crime, and to arrest the supposed wrongdoer. Although intended to be the means of recovering stolen property, search and seizure was commonly used to find books, letters, and other material that would show the occupant to be an opponent of the government. The seized materials were then used when the occupant of the house was brought to trial.

As a result of struggles that extended over many years, British

[27]

monarchs were forced to accept the idea that "a house is the occupant's castle." Thereafter, officers of the king or queen were required to go before a judge, explain under oath why a particular building should be searched, and ask for a warrant, or court order, which authorized entry into that house alone. Only when armed with a search warrant that described the property to be entered, and the persons and things to be seized, could the officers proceed.

To prevent misuse of the government's right to have a person's house searched, the Fourth Amendment placed this restraint on federal authority:

> *"The right of the people to be secure in their*
> *persons, houses, papers, and effects, against un-*
> *reasonable searches and seizures, shall not be*
> *violated, and no Warrants shall issue, but upon*
> *probable cause, supported by Oath or affirmation,*
> *and particularly describing the place to be*
> *searched, and the persons or things to be seized."*

THE FIFTH AMENDMENT

Through the centuries, the British developed a system for protecting the rights of persons accused of crime. For example, a civilian, or nonmilitary person, charged with armed robbery, murder, or other serious offense could not be brought to trial without the order of a grand (French for "large") jury. This group of from sixteen to twenty-three citizens was chosen from among the taxpayers of the district in which a judge conducted court. The grand jury's job was to consider the evidence of wrongdoing that officers of the government laid before it. After considering the facts in the case, the grand jury decided whether or not to issue an indictment, or order to stand trial. Requiring a group of respected citizens to weigh the evidence before an accused person could be tried protected the individual from hasty, improper action on the part of the government.

The Fifth Amendment requires a grand-jury
indictment before a civilian can be brought to
trial for a serious offense under federal law.

After a person was indicted by a grand jury, the accused was tried by a petit (French for "small") jury. This jury was made up of twelve citizens, again chosen from among the taxpayers of a court district. After hearing the evidence submitted by the officials of the government and by the defense, the jury gave its verdict, or decision. If found innocent of the charges, the accused was acquitted, or freed. In case the jury found the party guilty, the judge who conducted the trial fixed the sentence according to law.

But sometimes the royal government was determined to place a person behind bars. After having been tried and found not guilty by a jury, he or she might be arrested and tried again for the same offense. This was known as placing a person in double jeopardy. It was a practice long opposed in England and in the American colonies.

The Fifth Amendment prohibits the
federal government from trying a person
more than once for the same offense.

The First Amendment protects an individual's right to speak freely. The Fifth Amendment protects an individual's right to remain

[29]

silent. This guarantee is expressed in the statement that no one may be compelled to testify, or make a statement, when being tried on criminal charges.

The guarantee brings to mind times when government officials tried to compel accused persons to bear witness against themselves. Confessions were often forced by questioning the prisoner for so many hours that resistance was broken. All too frequently the prisoner was tortured in an effort to secure a confession.

An accused person's right to silence is also a reminder of an important principle, or rule, of English and American law: an individual charged with a crime is not required to prove his or her innocence. Instead it is the government's responsibility to prove that the accused person is guilty beyond a reasonable doubt.

The Fifth Amendment protects an
accused person's right to remain silent.

As a further protection for those accused of wrongdoing, the Fifth Amendment forbids the federal government to execute, imprison, or take the property of a person without "due process of law." The exact meaning of that phrase has bothered judges and experts on civil rights since it was first placed in the Constitution. At the time the Bill of Rights was adopted, "due process of law" generally was considered to mean that punishment must be reasonable, and that it may be given only after the accused person has had a fair trial.

The government's right to take a person's property so that it may be used for a courthouse, highway, school, or other public purpose has been recognized for centuries. But the understanding always has been that the government will pay the private owner a fair price for anything that is taken. When the property owner and the government cannot agree, the dispute must be settled in court.

The Fifth Amendment permits the federal government
to take private property only when two conditions
are met: the property must be for the use of the pub-
lic, and the owner must be paid a fair price for it.

THE SIXTH AMENDMENT

Both the history of England and the history of the American colonies provide many examples of the unfair treatment of persons accused of crime. Under some British monarchs, it was common practice to place someone under arrest without giving a reason. The person might then be put in prison and kept there for a long time before being brought to trial. Often the accused was tried in secret, and was not allowed to hear the witnesses who supported the charges brought by the government. Frequently the accused did not have the assistance of a lawyer. The person accused of crime was placed at a further disadvantage because a judge appointed by the king or queen conducted the trial, ruled on points of law, decided the facts in the case, declared the verdict, and determined the punishment.

Over a period of many years, the British developed the jury system as a means of correcting some of the abuses described. The right to trial by jury was based upon the belief that it was fairer to have a group of ordinary citizens weigh the evidence and decide the facts in the case than to let a judge have the entire responsibility for a trial. And so it became the custom for judges to preside over a trial and explain points of law when necessary. The trial jury heard the evidence and reached a verdict. It was the judge's task to determine the sentence when the jury declared that the accused party was guilty.

[31]

The Sixth Amendment requires trials to be held in public, and as soon as possible after the grand jury indicts a person. The trial must take place in the area where the crime supposedly occurred, so that the accused will have less difficulty in securing witnesses who may be able to support his or her defense. Moreover, the accused party must have the opportunity to challenge the witnesses who support the government's charges. As a final protection, a person accused of a federal crime must have a lawyer to assist in securing justice.

The Sixth Amendment safeguards the rights of an accused person when brought to trial on criminal charges.

THE SEVENTH AMENDMENT

The Sixth Amendment provides for trial by jury in *criminal* cases. These cases develop when a person is accused of counterfeiting money, kidnapping, or another criminal offense under federal law. In a criminal case, the government is the injured party because it accuses some person of breaking its laws. The government brings charges against the accused, attempts to prove the person's guilt, and inflicts punishment when a guilty verdict is reached by the trial jury.

The Seventh Amendment provides for trial by jury in certain kinds of *civil* cases. In this type of case, a private citizen takes action as an injured party. The claim is based upon the harm supposedly done by another party to the person or property of the man or woman who takes action. The party claiming the injury sues, or "takes to court," the person who is accused of causing the loss, to force him or her to pay damages or otherwise make up for the injury caused. In civil cases,

Jury hearing members tour the site of the May 1970 Kent State shootings, in which four people were killed.

the government acts something like an umpire. It provides the court where disputes between private parties can be settled, and enforces the terms of settlement determined by the judge after the jury has rendered its decision.

The Seventh Amendment provides for trial by jury in certain types of civil cases.

THE EIGHTH AMENDMENT

When a person charged with a crime awaits trial, a judge may release the accused on bail. That is, the judge may agree to let the party charged with the crime remain free until the day the trial begins. But to make sure that the accused person shows up, the judge usually requires the posting of a bond, or money guarantee. This means that whoever provides the bail bond must agree to forfeit, or give up, the amount of money that the judge sets, in case the accused person fails to appear in court for the trial. The amount of money that the judge requires as bail depends in large measure upon the seriousness of the crime that the person is accused of committing. However, the Eighth Amendment forbids a federal judge to require an excessive, or unnecessarily large, amount of bail. The same restriction applies when a judge imposes a fine, or sum of money that is to be paid as punishment.

At the time the Bill of Rights was added to the Constitution, there were many Americans who either had seen or had heard about the cruel kinds of punishment imposed by a judge. Having a hand cut off or an eye put out was punishment suffered by some convicted criminals. Whipping and branding were more common types of penalties.

The Eighth Amendment protects persons accused
of crime in these words: "Excessive bail shall
not be required, nor excessive fines imposed,
nor cruel and unusual punishments inflicted."

THE NINTH AMENDMENT

James Madison and other leaders who drew up the Bill of Rights did not want anyone to believe that the people of the United States had only those rights described in the first eight amendments. Accordingly, the Ninth Amendment states that Americans retained certain privileges when they established the federal government. Among the numerous rights retained by the people are the just claim to privacy, and the right to engage in political activity.

THE TENTH AMENDMENT

The last of the amendments that make up the Bill of Rights is yet another reminder that the Constitutional Convention set up a federal government of limited authority. The federal government was to have only those powers described in the Constitution—such as the right to coin money, to regulate commerce between states, and to wage war against other nations.

The Tenth Amendment makes it clear that when the states agreed to the Union, they retained many powers. These included maintaining public schools, regulating marriage and divorce, and providing for public health and safety.

The Tenth Amendment also emphasizes the fact that the Constitution withholds certain powers both from the federal government and from the governments of the separate states. Powers denied each type of government are described both in the body of the Constitution and in its amendments.

WHO DETERMINES
THE MEANING
OF THE WORDS?

Earl Warren, a former Chief Justice of the United States Supreme Court, once referred to the Bill of Rights as the most precious part of the system of law that we inherited from our ancestors. The Chief Justice pointed out that the Bill of Rights has only 462 words. He then went on to say that through the years millions of words have been written about the few words of the Bill of Rights itself.

Since the first ten amendments were added to the Constitution,* countless Americans have interpreted, or explained, their meaning. The most important interpretations have been those of Congress, the President, and the federal courts. Members of each branch of government have read the few words in a particular amendment, decided upon their meaning, and then acted accordingly. The wide differences of opinion are shown in these interpretations placed upon the section of the First Amendment that deals with religion. President Jefferson said that the First Amendment built a wall of separation between the church and the government. Because of that belief, Jefferson would not even set aside a day for national prayer and fasting. Later on, Congress took a much broader view of the First Amendment. For example, Congress decided that public funds could be used to buy

*U.S. Supreme Court Chief Justice Earl Warren
was an important interpreter of the Bill of Rights.*

equipment and nonreligious books for pupils who go to parochial, or church-supported schools, as well as for those who attend public schools.

Some of the most far-reaching interpretations of the church-government section of the First Amendment have been made by the Supreme Court. The Court interpreted the words dealing with the relations between the church and the government to mean that no government in the United States can set up a church, or pass laws that aid any religion. No government can force or influence "a person to go to or to remain away from a church against his will or force him to profess a belief or disbelief in any religion. . . . No tax in any amount, large or small, can be levied to support any religious activities or institutions. . . . Neither a state nor the Federal Government can, openly or secretly, participate in the affairs of any religious organization. . . ."

These examples call attention to the fact that the three branches of government often have conflicting interpretations of the Bill of Rights. In such instances, the Supreme Court is the final authority on the meaning of the words.

FREEDOM: COMPLETE OR LIMITED?

The Bill of Rights has been interpreted by the President, the Congress, and the federal courts from the time it was added to the Constitution until this very moment. A few public officials have argued that the rights described in the first ten amendments are absolute. That is, they are unrestricted, and no limitations may be placed upon them by any government. This position was taken by a noted member of the Supreme Court, Justice Hugo Black, as well as by several other authorities on the Constitution.

For the most part, the Supreme Court and other interpreters of the Constitution have successfully claimed that the rights described in the first ten amendments are relative. That is, the time and the conditions under which a right is claimed may cause restrictions to be placed upon it. For example, as Supreme Court Justice Holmes observed, freedom of speech does not permit a person to shout "Fire!" in a crowded theater when there is no fire. Also, one person's right must always be considered in relation to the rights of others: one man's freedom to swing his arm ends where the other man's nose begins.

In looking back over American history, one finds that freedom of speech is curbed, or checked, whenever the nation is at war or is seemingly threatened with war. At such times, the President, the Congress, and even the Supreme Court argue that peacetime freedom must give way to wartime restrictions. For example, when criticized for the curbs he placed on freedom of speech and other rights during the Civil War, President Lincoln had this to say: "Since these rebels are violating the Constitution in order to destroy the Union, I will violate the Constitution, if necessary, to save the Union."

The right to criticize the government in time of war was restricted by Congress during World War I with laws aimed at anyone opposed to American participation in the conflict. World War II brought more severe restrictions on freedom of speech, particularly on the freedom of those accused of being opposed to the war effort. But it was the "Cold War" of the 1950s that led to the most criticized curbs on freedom of speech. During that time, the Soviet Union was considered the chief enemy of the United States. Members of the Communist party in this country were accused of supporting the enemy.

In 1949, these Communist leaders were appealing their convictions by claiming their First Amendment rights had been violated.

Congress passed a number of laws that denied American Communists the right to speak freely. In upholding laws aimed at members of the Communist party in the United States, the Supreme Court declared that it was permissible for Communist leaders to urge other people to accept their beliefs. But it was illegal to urge other people to bring about change by force or violence. As a result of Supreme Court decisions, Communist leaders in this country were imprisoned.

In upholding curbs on freedom of speech, the Supreme Court made many Americans unhappy. Among this group were several Supreme Court justices who disagreed with the majority decisions. (Supreme Court decisions are determined by a majority vote of its nine members. Justices who disagree with the majority usually write a dissenting, or minority, opinion in which they state their reasons for reaching a different view than the one stated in the official ruling of the Court. Frequently, a dissenting opinion becomes better known than the majority decision because of the brilliance of its argument. Moreover, a dissenting opinion written in one period of American history sometimes becomes the basis for a majority opinion in a later period, as two cases mentioned later in the chapter will bear out. This feature of the Supreme Court shows that it is influenced by public opinion, and that it changes with the times.)

Critics of the Supreme Court in the cases relating to Communism pointed out that the First Amendment was intended to be a safeguard for persons who were attempting to spread ideas that were unpopular at the time. In depriving Americans of the right to hear opposing opinions, the Supreme Court had made it impossible for citizens to find the truth by looking at all sides of a question. Furthermore, in silencing a handful of Communists, the Supreme Court had made it easier to silence other groups whose views were unpopular. To put it another way, a weapon used against one group might be used against another.

If that happened, democracy might give way to dictatorship—a system in which the government allows no disagreement with its policies.

THREATS TO FREEDOM

Like freedom of speech, freedom of the press is also subject to restrictions. For example, freedom of the press does not include the right to libel. (As noted earlier, libel is the publication of words or pictures that damage a person's reputation or hold the person up to ridicule.) Moreover, Congress has placed certain restrictions on the radio-television programs, books, magazines, and motion pictures that are offered to the public. Most of these restrictions have to do with the distribution of material that may be considered obscene or pornographic. These words describe books, TV programs, movies, and magazines that deal with sex in such a way that many people are offended. Obscenity presents a great problem to government officials because what one person considers a fine book or motion picture, another person considers filthy trash. A nude figure that one individual regards as art may strike another viewer as indecent.

The Supreme Court has had a hard time in dealing with obscenity because the justices themselves are as divided on the subject as the American people are. However, the Court now recognizes the right of state governments to forbid the distribution of books, magazines, and motion pictures that a majority of the residents of a local community consider indecent. But since many people believe that any restriction on what they may see and hear violates the Bill of Rights, they continue to challenge all rulings on obscenity. For that reason, it appears certain that the Supreme Court will be hearing cases dealing with obscenity for many years to come.

The Constitution forbids the federal government to deprive anyone of property, liberty, or life without a fair trial. But in time of war these rights are always restricted and sometimes denied. A good example is the treatment received by Americans of Japanese ancestry upon the outbreak of World War II. Without any test of their loyalty to their government, more than 70,000 native-born Japanese-American citizens were forcibly removed from their homes on the West Coast and confined in detention camps. Many defenders of civil liberties protested when thousands of American citizens were imprisoned without trial, but the Supreme Court upheld the policy of the federal government. Many years later, President Ford made a public statement in which he acknowledged that an injustice had been done Japanese-American citizens.

Scientific discoveries have given new meaning to that part of the Fourth Amendment that forbids unreasonable searches and seizures. Means have been developed to search a home or place of business without the occupant knowing it. Conversations may be overheard by tapping telephones, installing hidden microphones, or placing outside a room hearing devices that are sensitive enough to pick up conversations through the walls. Tiny microphones, recording devices, and cameras may be concealed so that the unsuspecting occupant of a building reveals many secrets to the "invader" who has violated the person's privacy.

Above: During World War II Japanese-Americans were considered enemy aliens. Below: This Japanese-American serviceman had to visit his family in an Idaho relocation center where they were being held.

*Clarence Kelley was FBI Director in 1976,
when Congress was investigating
charges of illegal activities by the bureau.*

Congress responded to the new threat to privacy by requiring federal officials to secure a court order before engaging in what may be described as electronic search and seizure. But while some federal agencies have obeyed the law, others have ignored it. Members of Congress finally became so alarmed at the violation of the law that an investigation of the Central Intelligence Agency (CIA), the Federal Bureau of Investigation (FBI), and other government intelligence agencies was held in 1976. The congressional committee made some amazing discoveries. Acting illegally, government intelligence agencies had opened several hundred thousand letters that had been mailed to private persons or organizations, had read and copied millions of overseas messages, placed more than ten thousand wiretaps and "bugs," and committed hundreds of acts of burglary.

After describing the way in which government intelligence agencies had violated the Fourth Amendment, an editorial in *The New York Times* called upon Congress and the President to force the CIA, FBI, and other intelligence agencies to obey the law. But the editorial pointed out that in the end, the people of the United States will determine whether the Fourth Amendment will be respected or not. The final outcome, the editorial concluded, "will depend more on whether as a people we believe in freedom or fear it."

NEW FREEDOM FOR AMERICANS

Sometimes a thoughtful person becomes discouraged about the Bill of Rights. It seems that the civil liberties described there are ignored as often as they are observed. But good news is not hard to find. For one thing, the Bill of Rights has been strengthened over a period of years. Some writers on the Constitution say that the Bill of Rights now consists of sixteen amendments, rather than the original ten. The three amendments added at the end of the Civil War extended freedom to millions of black Americans. The THIRTEENTH brought an end to slavery. The FOURTEENTH guaranteed equal treatment before the law. The FIFTEENTH gave black Americans the right to vote.

Considerably more than half the population of the United States reached a long-sought goal when women (NINETEENTH AMENDMENT) and young people between the ages of eighteen and twenty-one (TWENTY-SIXTH AMENDMENT) gained the right to vote. Before the adoption of the TWENTY-FOURTH AMENDMENT, millions of poor Americans were barred from voting because they could not pay the tax that a number of states required as the price of casting a ballot. When the poll tax was abolished, or removed, millions of disadvantaged Americans gained the privilege of voting. Now a great effort is being made to add the EQUAL RIGHTS AMENDMENT to the Constitution. As its title indicates, the amendment would guarantee equal treatment for all Americans, regardless of their sex. For example, the adoption of the Equal Rights Amendment would make unconstitutional all discrimination against women in employment and other aspects of life.

The Bill of Rights has been extended not only by constitutional amendment, but also by acts of Congress, presidential orders, and decisions of federal courts. Thus the Supreme Court greatly extended the Bill of Rights in several decisions that it handed down in the 1920s and 1930s. The Court ruled that all the guarantees of the First Amendment and the most important guarantees of the other amendments apply to the states, as well as to the federal government. In this way, the Supreme Court made a major change in American government. The

Black people were granted the right to vote by the Fifteenth Amendment.

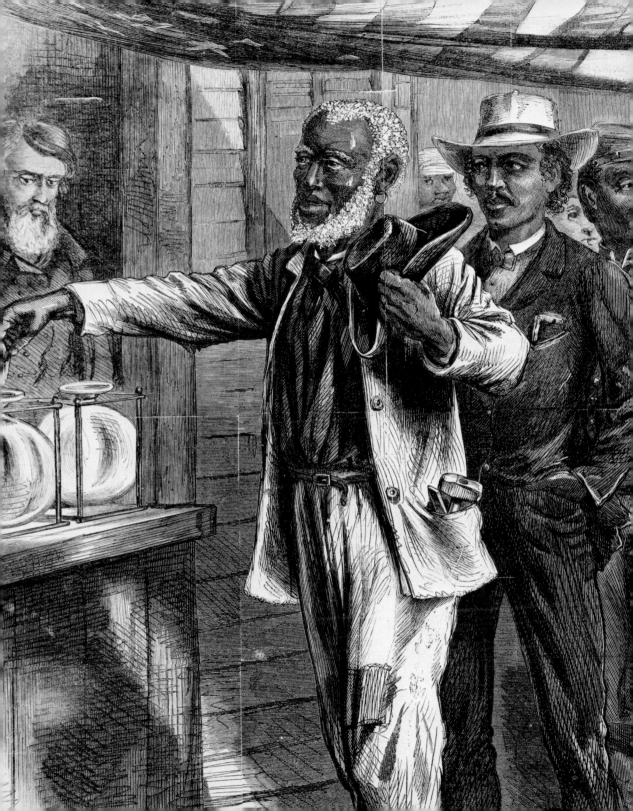

*Women demanded the right to vote, which
they received with the Nineteenth Amendment.*

Bill of Rights—originally intended as a check on the federal government—became a curb on the states as well. The Supreme Court's new interpretation of the Bill of Rights had the effect of forcing many reluctant state officials to end the unequal treatment of minority groups in the United States.

Other federal court decisions have widened the protection offered by the Bill of Rights in recent years. For example, the phrase "due process of law" has been interpreted to mean more than the fair and reasonable treatment of a person accused of breaking the law. The courts have gone beyond this earlier interpretation of the Fifth Amendment by ruling that the law itself must be fair and reasonable.

Another important change in the interpretation of the Bill of Rights has taken place in this century. In the period between the Civil War and World War I, federal courts showed more interest in protecting the rights of people to their property than in protecting freedom of speech, freedom of the press, and other civil liberties. In recent years, however, the protection of human rights has become a major concern of federal judges.

In 1896, the Supreme Court handed down one of its most famous decisions, *Plessy* v. *Ferguson.* The court ruled that it was constitutional to separate blacks and whites when they traveled in railroad cars, as long as the accommodations were equal. The decision implied that it was equally constitutional to segregate the races in schools, theaters, and other public facilities.

In opposing the majority decision, Justice John Marshall Harlan pointed out that separate facilities were never equal. What the Court had actually done was to give its blessing to the unequal treatment of black Americans. In disagreeing with the majority, Justice Harlan made a statement that is often quoted: "The Constitution is color-blind, and neither knows nor tolerates classes among citizens. In respect of civil rights, all citizens are equal before the law."

A grandson and namesake of the same justice who had disagreed with the majority in 1896 was a justice of the Supreme Court in 1954, when the high court handed down another historic decision, *Brown* v. *Board of Education of Topeka*. In that case, all nine justices agreed that segregated schools were unconstitutional. In effect, the Supreme Court in 1954 reversed the decision the Court made in 1896. This new decision brought vast changes in the North as well as the South. Public officials in many parts of the nation challenged the Supreme Court ruling. A very dramatic showdown came when Governor Orval Faubus of Arkansas refused to obey a federal court order to bring an end to segregated schools in Little Rock, the state capital. President Dwight Eisenhower sent federal troops to enforce the court order. The Bill of Rights was strengthened, this time by presidential action.

Even more far-reaching than Supreme Court decisions were the laws dealing with civil rights that Congress passed in the 1960s. The black American's right to vote, guaranteed by the Fifteenth Amendment almost a century before, was finally made real in the Voting Rights Act of 1965. Laws requiring equal treatment in education, housing, and employment were also passed in an effort to give black Americans the same opportunities provided to white citizens. In short, Congress gave new "muscle" to the Bill of Rights.

There was a very important reason for the changed view of the Bill of Rights taken by Congress, the President, and the federal courts in the 1960s. Government officials were responding to changes that had taken place in the thinking of millions of Americans. Countless citizens, black and white alike, had come to the conclusion that inequality was no longer acceptable in a democratic country such as the United States. Having made that decision, leaders of both races set up organi-

"Separate but equal" facilities for
blacks were ruled unconstitutional.

zations that made full use of the First Amendment right to pressure the government to provide equal treatment for all citizens. Members of Congress, the President, and federal judges were impressed when almost half a million Americans gathered in Washington one day in 1963 to demand civil rights laws. Federal officials were likewise impressed when individual citizens, including Rev. Martin Luther King, Jr., laid down their lives in defense of civil liberties.

Like Elijah P. Lovejoy, these new martyrs reminded their fellow citizens of a very important fact. Whether the Bill of Rights is respected depends more upon individual Americans than upon the government itself. It is often *people,* and not *governments,* that deprive a person of freedom. Elijah P. Lovejoy's rights were taken from him by his fellow citizens—who first denied him the right to publish his newspaper, and then deprived him of his life. And it was Lovejoy's supporters, first in Illinois, and then throughout the nation, who brought an end to slavery and made the Bill of Rights apply to Americans of all races.

Many years after Lovejoy died, one of the most notable of all federal judges, Learned Hand, warned citizens of the United States that the future of the Bill of Rights depended more upon them than upon their government. "Liberty lies in the hearts of men and women; when it dies there, no constitution, no law, no court can save it; no constitution, no law, no court can even do much to help it. While it lies there, it needs no constitution, no law, no court to save it."

Above: Civil rights demonstrators in the 1960s, in Montgomery, Alabama. Below: The Reverend Martin Luther King, Jr., speaking during the 1963 civil rights demonstration in Washington, defended civil liberties until his death.

GLOSSARY

Acquit Decision reached in court that an accused party is not guilty of the charges brought.

Amendment Changes made in the main part of a constitution or law, or an addition placed at the end.

Bail Money deposited with a court to guarantee the appearance of an accused person on the day of trial.

Bill of Attainder Punishment of a person by act of the legislature, rather than as a result of conviction after trial.

Chief Executive Head of the law-enforcing branch of government.

Civil Liberties Personal and property rights guaranteed by a constitution or basic law.

Congress Lawmaking body of the federal government.

Constitution Document, or written statement, that describes the framework of government and the principles on which it operates.

Double Jeopardy Term applying to persons tried twice for the same offense under the same system of law.

Established Church Religious body officially connected with the government and receiving assistance from it.

[56]

Executive The law-enforcing branch of government.

Ex Post Facto Term describing punishment for an act that was not criminal when committed.

Federal Term applying to a union made up of separate state governments and an overall national government.

Grand Jury Group of citizens who hear evidence of crime gathered by the government for the purpose of determining whether an accused person should be held for trial.

Habeas Corpus Court order requiring officer who is detaining someone to bring the prisoner before a judge and give reasons for the detention.

Indictment Written statement of grand jury charging one or more parties with having committed a crime.

Judiciary System of courts.

Legislature Lawmaking branch of government.

Libel Publishing articles or pictures that injure a person's reputation or hold him up to ridicule.

Parliament Legislative or lawmaking body, in England consisting of the House of Lords and the House of Commons.

Petit Jury Group of twelve persons who determine the guilt or innocence of the accused after listening to evidence submitted at a trial.

Prime Minister Leader of the British Parliament and head of the executive department of government.

Ratify To accept or approve.

Search Warrant Court order authorizing the search of a particular building, and the seizure of persons or articles that are described.

Treason Betrayal of one's country.

Verdict Decision reached by a trial jury.

Veto An executive's refusal to approve an act passed by the legislature.

[57]

THE BILL OF RIGHTS
OF THE CONSTITUTION

**ARTICLES IN ADDITION TO, AND
AMENDMENT OF, THE CONSTITUTION
OF THE UNITED STATES OF AMERICA,
PROPOSED BY CONGRESS, AND
RATIFIED BY THE SEVERAL STATES,
PURSUANT TO THE FIFTH ARTICLE
OF THE ORIGINAL CONSTITUTION.**

AMENDMENT I

Congress shall make no law respecting an establishment of religion, or prohibiting the free exercise thereof; or abridging the freedom of speech, or of the press; or the right of the people peaceably to assemble, and to petition the Government for a redress of grievances.

AMENDMENT II

A well regulated Militia, being necessary to the security of a free State, the right of the people to keep and bear Arms, shall not be infringed.

[58]

AMENDMENT III

No Soldier shall, in time of peace be quartered in any house, without the consent of the Owner, nor in time of war, but in a manner to be prescribed by law.

AMENDMENT IV

The right of the people to be secure in their persons, houses, papers, and effects, against unreasonable searches and seizures, shall not be violated, and no Warrants shall issue, but upon probable cause, supported by Oath or affirmation, and particularly describing the place to be searched, and the persons or things to be seized.

AMENDMENT V

No person shall be held to answer for a capital, or otherwise infamous crime, unless on a presentment or indictment of a Grand Jury, except in cases arising in the land or naval forces, or in the Militia, when in actual service in time of War or public danger; nor shall any person be subject for the same offence to be twice put in jeopardy of life or limb; nor shall be compelled in any criminal case to be a witness against himself, nor be deprived of life, liberty, or property, without due process of law; nor shall private property be taken for public use,   . without just compensation.

AMENDMENT VI

In all criminal prosecutions, the accused shall enjoy the right to a speedy and public trial, by an impartial jury of the State and district wherein the crime shall have been committed, which district shall have been previously ascertained by law, and to be informed of the nature and cause of the accusation; to be confronted with the witnesses against him; to have compulsory process for obtaining witnesses in his favor, and to have the Assistance of Counsel for his defence.

AMENDMENT VII

In Suits at common law, where the value in controversy shall exceed twenty dollars, the right of trial by jury shall be preserved, and no fact tried by a jury, shall be otherwise re-examined in any Court of the United States, than according to the rules of the common law.

AMENDMENT VIII

Excessive bail shall not be required, nor excessive fines imposed, nor cruel and unusual punishments inflicted.

AMENDMENT IX

The enumeration in the Constitution, of certain rights, shall not be construed to deny or disparage others retained by the people.

AMENDMENT X

The powers not delegated to the United States by the Constitution, nor prohibited by it to the States, are reserved to the States respectively, or to the people.

BIBLIOGRAPHY

Asch, Sidney H., *Civil Rights and Responsibilities*. New York: Arco
   Publishing Company, 1968.

Beecher, Edward, *Narrative of Riots at Alton*. Alton, Illinois: George
   Holton, 1838.

Brant, Irving, *The Bill of Rights*. Indianapolis: Bobbs-Merrill Company, Inc., 1965.

Burns, James M., and Jack Walter Peltason, *Government of the People*.
   Englewood Cliffs, N.J.: Prentice-Hall, Inc., 1964.

Cushman, Robert E., *Leading Constitutional Decisions*. New York:
   Appleton-Century-Crofts, 1971.

Ferguson, John H., and Dean E. McHenry, *The American System of
   Government*. New York: McGraw-Hill Book Company, 1971.

Harris, Robert J., *The Quest for Equality*. Baton Rouge: Louisiana
   State University Press, 1960.

Kauper, Paul G., *Civil Liberties and the Constitution*. Ann Arbor: University of Michigan Press, 1962.

Morison, Samuel Eliot, *Oxford History of the American People*. New
   York: Oxford University Press, 1965.

[61]

Rogge, O. John, *The First and the Fifth.* New York: Thomas Nelson & Sons, 1960.

Saye, Albert B., *American Constitutional Law.* Columbus, Ohio: Charles E. Merrill Publishing Company, 1975.

Schwartz, Bernard, *The Law in America.* New York: American Heritage Publishing Co., Inc., 1974.

Tresolini, Rocco J., *American Constitutional Law.* New York: Macmillan Company, 1965.

Westin, Alan F., *Privacy and Freedom.* New York: Atheneum Publishers, 1970.

INDEX

[64]

[65]

ABOUT THE AUTHOR

E. B. Fincher has been both a student and a teacher of history and political science. As a student, he received his master's degree from Columbia University in New York City, and his doctorate from New York University. He has taught in both junior high school and college. E. B. Fincher is the author of five textbooks and two general books, all in the area of history and political science. A man of many interests, he lives on a farm in Asbury, New Jersey, where he raises sheep and grows ornamental evergreens.

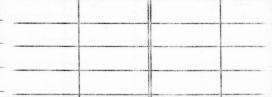